In the Park

Written by Mary Ashby
Illustrated by Josephine Martin

Collins *Educational*
An imprint of HarperCollins *Publishers*

It's morning. The park is empty.
There are no people, no dogs, no cats.

Only a bird singing its morning song
at the top of a tall tree.

But wait! There is something else.
Something sliding along slowly beside the path.

It has a hard shell.
It moves by sliding along on its foot.
It can pull its body inside its shell.
It has four feelers that it can pull right
inside its head.

What can it be?

It's a snail.

It's morning. The park is empty.
There are no people, no dogs, no cats.
Only a bird singing its morning song
at the top of a tall tree,
and a slow snail beside the path.

But wait! There is something else.
Something on the railings.

It has a rounded body.
It has a white cross on its back.
It has eight legs with stripes
on them.
It has eight eyes.

What can it be?

7

It's a garden spider.

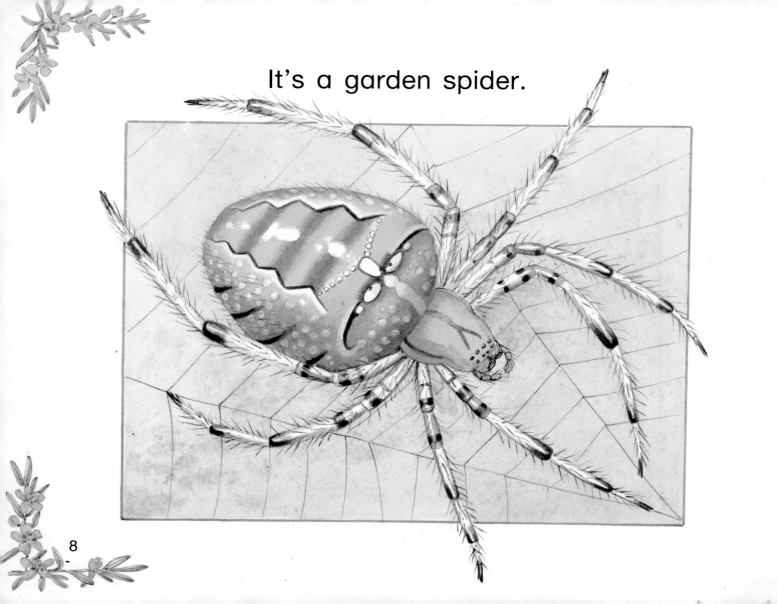

It's morning and the park is empty.
There are no people, no dogs, no cats.
Only a bird singing its morning song
at the top of a tall tree,
a slow snail beside the path,
and a garden spider in her web on the railings.

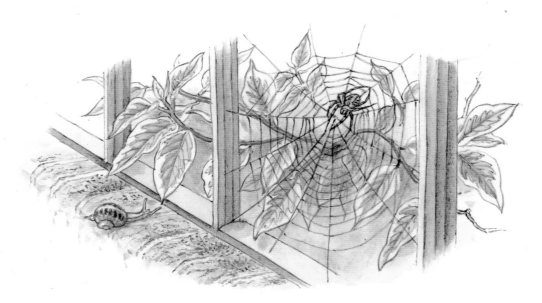

9

But wait!
There is something else.
Something hiding in a rose.

It has six legs.
Its back is hard and shiny,
and as green as grass.
It has two wings to fly with.
It has two short antennae.

What can it be?

It's a rose beetle.

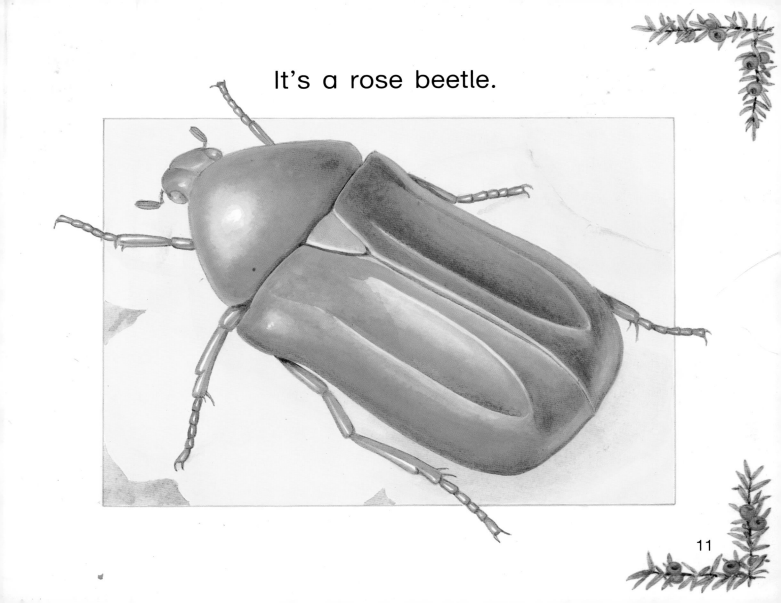

It's morning.

The park is empty.

There is only a bird singing its morning song
at the top of a tall tree,

a slow snail beside the path,

a garden spider in her web on the railings,

and a rose beetle hiding in a rose.

But wait!

There is something else.

Something chirping softly in the grass.

It has six legs.
Its back legs are very long and strong for jumping.
It has long wings folded along its back.
When it rubs its back legs against its wings it makes a soft chirping noise.

What can it be?

It's a grasshopper.

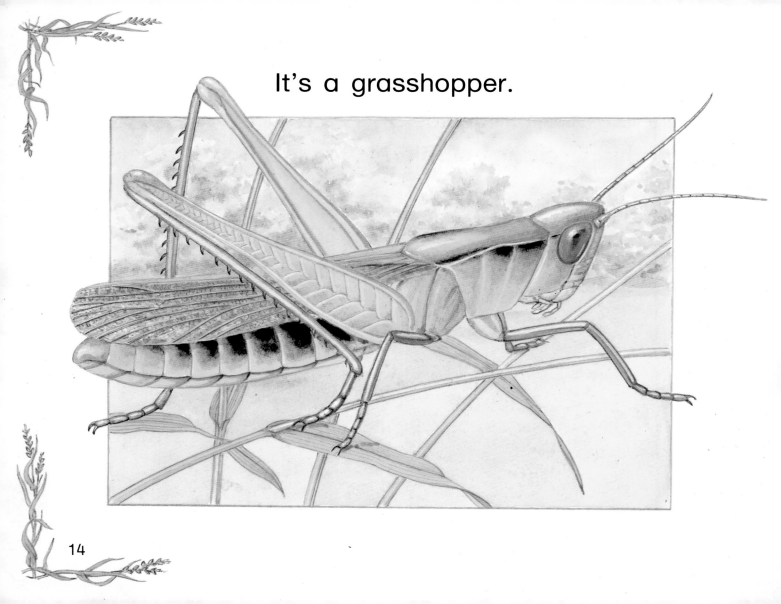

It is morning in the park.
There are no people, or dogs, or cats.
But there is a bird singing its morning song
at the top of a tall tree,

a slow snail beside the path,

a garden spider in her web on the railings,

a rose beetle hiding in a rose,

a grasshopper chirping in the grass, and...

Me, in the park, in the morning.